M O M E N T S
O F
S I L E N C E

52 Weekly Exercises for the Christian Mind, Body, and Soul

Mitch,

Praying that your moments of
silence are, holy, thought-provoking,
and beneficial

Peace and all good things
Kevin

Kevin Jurek

Table of Contents

Introduction

Mind

"Reflect on what I am saying, for the Lord
will give you understanding in everything."

2 Timothy 2:7

Soul

"Pray without ceasing."

1 Thessalonians 5:17

Body

"Do you not know that you are the temple of God,
and that the Spirit of God dwells in you?"

1 Corinthians 3:16

Have you ever watched or attended a sporting event that is being held shortly after the death of someone important to those in attendance or after some tragedy? Before the game begins, the stadium announcer asks the crowd to stand and observe "a moment of silence." Most people respect the request for silence, but I always wondered how many people in the crowd were actually thinking about or reflecting on the person or event that prompted the moment of silence in the first place. I'm sure that some do, but I'm betting that a lot of folks are just wondering, "When is this going to be over, so we can get this game started?"

How many times in your life have you called for your own personal moment of silence? If you're like me, it's probably not enough. That's the reason I wrote this book. I often thought about what Jesus did when He needed to think. Quite often, He retreated to a quiet place for His own moment of silence. I figured if it worked for Him, it might just work for me, so I started trying this on my own.

I walk my golden retriever, Sammy, every morning. It doesn't matter if it's raining, snowing, or if it's 10 degrees below 0. Sammy and I are walking partners and we always get our day started together. I decided that during my walks with Sammy, I'd have my own moment of silence. When we head out in the morning, our neighborhood is very quiet and very dark. Rather than my normal routine of planning out the upcoming day in my head as Sammy walked alongside me, I decided I'd try something different. I started clearing my head of all that I could, through prayer, prior to heading out of the house. Then, I planted a single thought inside my head as Sammy and I headed out the door. I'd think of things like, "How am I going to connect with my students today?" (I do leadership development training for a living) or "What can I do to better connect with that person at work?" I was amazed at how many answers just flowed into my head during our walks.

I then started expanding the time that I spent in silence. I conditioned myself to do this during my drive into work. Not the entire 40-minute commute, but large chunks of it. It was during one of these silent times when the idea that eventually became this book was presented to me by God.

I started talking about this "moment of silence" concept with my friend, co-worker, and running partner, Stacy. Stacy was the Wellness Coordinator for our office. Our runs would often be consumed by conversation and prayer. One day, I asked her if she'd like to try running in silence with me. She found that it helped her, too. Because we saw the power that this discipline had, we decided to try coming up with a list of questions we could use during our running sessions. We sat down and came up with a list of 52 of them, one for each week of the year. I wrote the questions and saved them on my hard drive.

Sadly, Stacy and her family moved to another part of the state, and the list went stale for me. It might have just stayed in my computer forever, but something happened that has helped the list come back to life. On October 31, 2016, I got news that I thought I'd never get. My position as our company's Leadership Development Specialist was being eliminated as of the end of that calendar year, four years before my wife and I were going to begin a well-planned, well-deserved early retirement. It was a complete shock to me. After some time, reflective prayer, and a half hour of yelling at God during my commute home that day, I decided (with His help) to end the pity party, get off my butt, and do something about the situation. I had the opportunity to seek other employment at my current company, but I asked myself, "What can I do to move forward with my life beyond corporate America?" For quite a while, I'd had a plan in my head for a business of my own where I could supply my leadership and team development services to the public instead of just within one company. Those plans came to me during many of my moments of silence over the period of about a year. That business is now up and running! (oi-solutions.com)

It was during one of these moments of silence that the idea for this book came about, too. I ran the idea past several people, and they all said that it would certainly be unique and something they would use. With their encouragement (and by the grace of God), I sat down and started putting it together.

Although it's critical for us to exercise our minds and souls, I also think it's important for all of us to exercise our bodies. You don't have to be an elite athlete to do this. Just as I found effective quiet time while walking my dog or running, you should also find a time when you're exercising to have your daily moment of silence. Think out of the box. If you're a runner, give yoga a shot sometime. If you aren't physically active, use this as an opportunity to get your body in motion. You might try mixing it up during your week (yoga one day, cardio the next). If you're not into any of the things written here, just go out for a walk with your dog or a friend!

My prayer is that this book is a living document that helps you to exercise your body, your mind, and your soul. Enjoy!

Peace and All Good Things,

Kevin Jurek

How to Use This Book

It's flexible. You can follow the structure of the book using
my suggestions below or venture out on your own. Here is how
I suggest going through the book:

At the beginning of your week (whatever day that is), open the
book to the page you want to work on that week. I suggest going
straight through from week 1 to week 52, but that's up to you.
Make sure to hit all 52 chapters during the course of your year.
Put the week's starting date at the top of the page.

For at least 5 days during that week:

1. Find a quiet place where you won't be distracted and clear
    your mind of clutter. Read the scripture passage for the week,
    as well as the corresponding reflection question(s).

2. Spend as much time as you can in silence with your God.
    Be open to what He is telling you. Keep a pencil and paper
    (or your electronic device) handy so you can record your
    thoughts as you reflect. Note: You'll find as you go along that
    you'll become more and more comfortable with the amount
    of time you spend in silence. Try starting out with 5 or 10
    minutes and go from there.

3. After your reflection time, write down what you need to on that week's page. Write down any action plans and prayers answered in the journal section at the back of the book. Remember, you may have prayers answered for something you did weeks ago, so make sure to record those, too.

4. Exercise your body. Do whatever you want to do. Just make sure to do it for a minimum of 20 minutes. Try using your exercise time as your silent time. That's when I get most of my thinking done!

Options

- Go through the book with other people at the same time. It could be with your spouse, a Bible study group, prayer group, support group, exercise class, or circle of friends. Introduce the question and be silent in each other's company. Maybe do some physical activity together. Share with the group what God told you during your moment of silence. Share your action plans and your prayers answered with them, too.

- Work in "virtual groups." You don't have to be physically in the same place to do this with others. For example, work on your weekly sheet with friends or relatives that live far away from you.

As you go through this process, make sure you share your thoughts and the results you're getting from your mind, soul, and body exercises. Maybe a prayer has been answered. Maybe your health has improved in some way. Your testimony may encourage others to conduct their own personal moments of silence.

MOMENTS
OF
SILENCE

52 Weekly Exercises for the Christian Mind, Body, and Soul

Kevin Jurek

Week 1

"Let your life be free from love of money but
be content with what you have, for he has said,
'I will never forsake you or abandon you.'"

Hebrews 13:5

What is this passage saying to me today?

Other scripture that can help me think about this:

Think about this during your moment of silence:

How do I need to be smarter with my money?

Where can I cut back on or eliminate spending?

What are some unnecessary "luxury" items in my life?

Am I charitable enough with my money?

What I'm learning during my moments of silence this week:

Given what I've learned from scripture and during my moments of silence this week, what am I going to do about it and when am I going to get it done (put it on a calendar if you need to)?

Take care of your body. What physical activities did you do this week?

Week 2

Date:

_____

"Two are better than one: They get a good wage for their toil.
If the one falls, the other will help the fallen one. But woe to the
solitary person! If that one should fall, there is no other to help."

Ecclesiastes 4:9-10

_____

What is this passage saying to me today?

Other scripture that can help me think about this:

Think about this during your moment of silence:

Who do I really need to call on the phone this week?

What do I need to tell him or her?

What I'm learning during my moments of silence this week:

Given what I've learned from scripture and during my moments of silence this week, what am I going to do about it and when am I going to get it done (put it on a calendar if you need to)?

Take care of your body. What physical activities did you do this week?

Week 3

Date:

_____

"So we are ambassadors for Christ, as if God
were appealing through us. We implore you on behalf
of Christ, be reconciled to God."

2 Corinthians 5:20

_____

What is this passage saying to me today?

Other scripture that can help me think about this:

Think about this during your moment of silence:

Who are the 3 most important people in my life?

At my 80th birthday party, what would I like to tell them?

What I'm learning during my moments of silence this week:

Given what I've learned from scripture and during my moments of silence this week, what am I going to do about it and when am I going to get it done (put it on a calendar if you need to)?

Take care of your body. What physical activities did you do this week?

Week 4

Date:
_____

"Behold, I stand at the door and knock. If anyone hears
my voice and opens the door, [then] I will enter his house
and dine with him, and he with me."

Revelation 3:20

_____

What is this passage saying to me today?

Other scripture that can help me think about this:

Think about this during your moment of silence:

With whom do I need to reconnect?

What I'm learning during my moments of silence this week:

Given what I've learned from scripture and during my moments of silence this week, what am I going to do about it and when am I going to get it done (put it on a calendar if you need to)?

Take care of your body. What physical activities did you do this week?

Week 5

Date:

"As they continued their journey he entered a village where
a woman whose name was Martha welcomed him. She had a sister
named Mary [who] sat beside the Lord at his feet listening to him
speak. Martha, burdened with much serving, came to him and
said, 'Lord, do you not care that my sister has left me by myself
to do the serving? Tell her to help me.' The Lord said to her in reply,
'Martha, Martha, you are anxious and worried about many things.
There is need of only one thing. Mary has chosen the better part
and it will not be taken from her.'"

Luke 10:38-42

What is this passage saying to me today?

Other scripture that can help me think about this:

Think about this during your moment of silence:

What areas of my life deserve more of my time?

Why haven't I given more time to these areas?

What I'm learning during my moments of silence this week:

Given what I've learned from scripture and during my moments of silence this week, what am I going to do about it and when am I going to get it done (put it on a calendar if you need to)?

Take care of your body. What physical activities did you do this week?

Week 6

Date:

"But the noble plan noble deeds,
and in noble deeds they persist."

Isaiah 32:8

What is this passage saying to me today?

Other scripture that can help me think about this:

Think about this during your moment of silence:

What are the things I should be doing in the next few years?

What's my plan?

What I'm learning during my moments of silence this week:

Given what I've learned from scripture and during my moments of silence this week, what am I going to do about it and when am I going to get it done (put it on a calendar if you need to)?

Take care of your body. What physical activities did you do this week?

Week 7

Date:

"Many are the plans of the human heart,
but it is the decision of the LORD that endures."

Proverbs 19:21

What is this passage saying to me today?

Other scripture that can help me think about this:

Think about this during your moment of silence:

What are my top 3 bucket list items?

What is holding me back from checking them off?

What I'm learning during my moments of silence this week:

Given what I've learned from scripture and during my moments of silence this week, what am I going to do about it and when am I going to get it done (put it on a calendar if you need to)?

Take care of your body. What physical activities did you do this week?

Week 8

_____

"Which of you wishing to construct a tower does not first sit down
and calculate the cost to see if there is enough for its completion?
Otherwise, after laying the foundation and finding himself unable
to finish the work the onlookers should laugh at him and say, 'This
one began to build but did not have the resources to finish.' Or what
king marching into battle would not first sit down and decide whether
with ten thousand troops he can successfully oppose another king
advancing upon him with twenty thousand troops? But if not, while
he is still far away, he will send a delegation to ask for peace terms."

Luke 14:28-32

_____

What is this passage saying to me today?

Other scripture that can help me think about this:

Think about this during your moment of silence:

What is one area of my life where I can be better organized?

Why is it important for me to be better organized in this area?

What I'm learning during my moments of silence this week:

Given what I've learned from scripture and during my moments of silence this week, what am I going to do about it and when am I going to get it done (put it on a calendar if you need to)?

Take care of your body. What physical activities did you do this week?

Week 9

Date:

"But early in the morning he arrived again in the temple area, and all the people started coming to him, and he sat down and taught them. Then the scribes and the Pharisees brought a woman who had been caught in adultery and made her stand in the middle. They said to him, 'Teacher, this woman was caught in the very act of committing adultery. Now in the law, Moses commanded us to stone such women. So what do you say?' They said this to test him, so that they could have some charge to bring against him. Jesus bent down and began to write on the ground with his finger. But when they continued asking him, he straightened up and said to them, 'Let the one among you who is without sin be the first to throw a stone at her.' Again he bent down and wrote on the ground. And in response, they went away one by one, beginning with the elders. So he was left alone with the woman before him. Then Jesus straightened up and said to her, 'Woman, where are they? Has no one condemned you?' She replied, 'No one, sir.' Then Jesus said, 'Neither do I condemn you. Go, [and] from now on do not sin any more.'"

John 8:2-11

What is this passage saying to me today?

Other scripture that can help me think about this:

Think about this during your moment of silence:

How have I "put people into boxes" by judging them?

What can I do to eliminate this?

What I'm learning during my moments of silence this week:

Given what I've learned from scripture and during my moments of silence this week, what am I going to do about it and when am I going to get it done (put it on a calendar if you need to)?

Take care of your body. What physical activities did you do this week?

Week 10

Date: _____

"Do not neglect to do good and to share what you have;
God is pleased by sacrifices of that kind."

Hebrews 13:16

What is this passage saying to me today?

Other scripture that can help me think about this:

Think about this during your moment of silence:

What in my life do I tend to take for granted?

Which of these things should I be sharing with others?

What I'm learning during my moments of silence this week:

Given what I've learned from scripture and during my moments of silence this week, what am I going to do about it and when am I going to get it done (put it on a calendar if you need to)?

Take care of your body. What physical activities did you do this week?

Week 11

Date: _____

_____

"For my thoughts are not your thoughts, nor are your ways
my ways—oracle of the LORD. For as the heavens are higher
than the earth, so are my ways higher than your ways,
my thoughts higher than your thoughts."

Isaiah 55:8-9

What is this passage saying to me today?

Other scripture that can help me think about this:

Think about this during your moment of silence:

What are the things in my life that I would like to control
but I know I can't?

What am I doing about that?

What I'm learning during my moments of silence this week:

Given what I've learned from scripture and during my moments of silence this week, what am I going to do about it and when am I going to get it done (put it on a calendar if you need to)?

Take care of your body. What physical activities did you do this week?

Week 12

Date:

"For God did not give us a spirit of cowardice
but rather of power and love and self-control."

2 Timothy 1:7

What is this passage saying to me today?

Other scripture that can help me think about this:

Think about this during your moment of silence:

What is my biggest or most harmful habit?

What is standing in the way of overcoming it?

What should I be doing about it?

What I'm learning during my moments of silence this week:

Given what I've learned from scripture and during my moments of silence this week, what am I going to do about it and when am I going to get it done (put it on a calendar if you need to)?

Take care of your body. What physical activities did you do this week?

Week 13

Date:

_____

"I have the strength for everything through
him who empowers me."

Philippians 4:13

_____

What is this passage saying to me today?

Other scripture that can help me think about this:

Think about this during your moment of silence:

What one activity (sport, hobby, etc.) have I always wanted to try?
What is holding me back from trying it?

What I'm learning during my moments of silence this week:

Given what I've learned from scripture and during my moments of silence this week, what am I going to do about it and when am I going to get it done (put it on a calendar if you need to)?

Take care of your body. What physical activities did you do this week?

Week 14

Date: _____

"...be renewed in the spirit of your minds, and put on the new self, created in God's way in righteousness and holiness of truth."

Ephesians 4:23-24

_____

What is this passage saying to me today?

Other scripture that can help me think about this:

Think about this during your moment of silence:

What should I be doing to enhance or advance my career?

If I'm not in the workforce, what am I doing to "stay sharp"?

What I'm learning during my moments of silence this week:

Given what I've learned from scripture and during my moments of silence this week, what am I going to do about it and when am I going to get it done (put it on a calendar if you need to)?

Take care of your body. What physical activities did you do this week?

Week 15

_____

"Now the Lord is the Spirit, and where the Spirit
of the Lord is, there is freedom."

2 Corinthians 3:17

_____

What is this passage saying to me today?

Other scripture that can help me think about this:

Think about this during your moment of silence:

What is my favorite travel destination?

What makes that place so appealing to me?

Where else do I want to visit?

What I'm learning during my moments of silence this week:

Given what I've learned from scripture and during my moments of silence this week, what am I going to do about it and when am I going to get it done (put it on a calendar if you need to)?

Take care of your body. What physical activities did you do this week?

Week 16

Date:

"He said to them, 'Go into the whole world
and proclaim the gospel to every creature.'"

Mark 16:15

What is this passage saying to me today?

Other scripture that can help me think about this:

Think about this during your moment of silence:

If I could take a trip anywhere to do volunteer work,
where would it be and what would I do?

What I'm learning during my moments of silence this week:

Given what I've learned from scripture and during my moments of silence this week, what am I going to do about it and when am I going to get it done (put it on a calendar if you need to)?

Take care of your body. What physical activities did you do this week?

Week 17

Date:
_____

"If it is displeasing to you to serve the LORD, choose today whom
you will serve, the gods your ancestors served beyond the River
or the gods of the Amorites in whose country you are dwelling.
As for me and my household, we will serve the LORD."

Joshua 24:15

_____

What is this passage saying to me today?

Other scripture that can help me think about this:

Think about this during your moment of silence:

Who or what do I worship?

Is this a good thing or a bad thing?

What I'm learning during my moments of silence this week:

Given what I've learned from scripture and during my moments of silence this week, what am I going to do about it and when am I going to get it done (put it on a calendar if you need to)?

Take care of your body. What physical activities did you do this week?

Week 18

Date: _____

"You are the light of the world.
A city set on a mountain cannot be hidden."

Matthew 5:14

What is this passage saying to me today?

Other scripture that can help me think about this:

Think about this during your moment of silence:

What influence can I have on changes happening
in the community, the nation, or the world?

What I'm learning during my moments of silence this week:

Given what I've learned from scripture and during my moments of silence this week, what am I going to do about it and when am I going to get it done (put it on a calendar if you need to)?

Take care of your body. What physical activities did you do this week?

Week 19

Date:

"If your brother sins [against you], go and tell him
his fault between you and him alone. If he listens to you,
you have won over your brother."

Matthew 18:15

What is this passage saying to me today?

Other scripture that can help me think about this:

Think about this during your moment of silence:

What is the biggest argument or misunderstanding that
I have experienced?

Have I resolved it? If so, how?

If not, how should I?

What I'm learning during my moments of silence this week:

Given what I've learned from scripture and during my moments of silence this week, what am I going to do about it and when am I going to get it done (put it on a calendar if you need to)?

Take care of your body. What physical activities did you do this week?

Week 20

Date:

"Do you not know that your body is a temple of the
Holy Spirit within you, whom you have from God, and
that you are not your own? For you have been purchased
at a price. Therefore, glorify God in your body."

1 Corinthians 6:19-20

What is this passage saying to me today?

Other scripture that can help me think about this:

Think about this during your moment of silence:

What areas of my physical health have I been neglecting?

Why? What can I do better?

What I'm learning during my moments of silence this week:

Given what I've learned from scripture and during my moments of silence this week, what am I going to do about it and when am I going to get it done (put it on a calendar if you need to)?

Take care of your body. What physical activities did you do this week?

Week 21

Date: _____

"Do not repay anyone evil for evil; be concerned
for what is noble in the sight of all. If possible,
on your part, live at peace with all."

Romans 12:17-18

What is this passage saying to me today?

Other scripture that can help me think about this:

Think about this during your moment of silence:

Who is someone I'm close to that I'd consider to be a negative person?
How can I improve my relationship with him or her?

What I'm learning during my moments of silence this week:

Given what I've learned from scripture and during my moments of silence this week, what am I going to do about it and when am I going to get it done (put it on a calendar if you need to)?

Take care of your body. What physical activities did you do this week?

Week 22

Date:
_____

"Shout with joy to the LORD, all the earth;
break into song; sing praise."

Psalms 98:4

_____

What is this passage saying to me today?

Other scripture that can help me think about this:

Think about this during your moment of silence:

What is my favorite type of music?

Why do I like it so much?

What other types of music can I listen to this week?

What I'm learning during my moments of silence this week:

Given what I've learned from scripture and during my moments of silence this week, what am I going to do about it and when am I going to get it done (put it on a calendar if you need to)?

Take care of your body. What physical activities did you do this week?

Week 23

Date: _____

"Then the LORD will guide you always and satisfy your thirst in parched places, will give strength to your bones and you shall be like a watered garden, like a flowing spring whose waters never fail."

Isaiah 58:11

What is this passage saying to me today?

Other scripture that can help me think about this:

Think about this during your moment of silence:

What gives me the most satisfaction in my life?

Is that thing good or harmful for me?

Am I getting as much of it as I need?

Am I getting too much?

What I'm learning during my moments of silence this week:

Given what I've learned from scripture and during my moments of silence this week, what am I going to do about it and when am I going to get it done (put it on a calendar if you need to)?

Take care of your body. What physical activities did you do this week?

Week 24

Date:
_____

"If someone who has worldly means sees a brother
in need and refuses him compassion, how can the
love of God remain in him?"

1 John 3:17

_____

What is this passage saying to me today?

Other scripture that can help me think about this:

Think about this during your moment of silence:

Who in my circle of friends could I be helping more?

How so?

What I'm learning during my moments of silence this week:

Given what I've learned from scripture and during my moments of silence this week, what am I going to do about it and when am I going to get it done (put it on a calendar if you need to)?

Take care of your body. What physical activities did you do this week?

Week 25

Date: _____

"Listen to counsel and receive instruction,
that you may eventually become wise."

Proverbs 19:20

What is this passage saying to me today?

Other scripture that can help me think about this:

Think about this during your moment of silence:

Who can I seek out as a mentor to help me achieve
one of my life goals?

What I'm learning during my moments of silence this week:

Given what I've learned from scripture and during my moments of silence this week, what am I going to do about it and when am I going to get it done (put it on a calendar if you need to)?

Take care of your body. What physical activities did you do this week?

Week 26

Date:

_____

"...let the greatest among you be as the youngest, and
the leader as the servant. For who is greater, the one seated
at the table or the one who serves? Is it not the one seated
at the table? I am among you as the one who serves."

Luke 22:26-27

_____

What is this passage saying to me today?

Other scripture that can help me think about this:

Think about this during your moment of silence:

What can I do to serve others more?

What I'm learning during my moments of silence this week:

Given what I've learned from scripture and during my moments of silence this week, what am I going to do about it and when am I going to get it done (put it on a calendar if you need to)?

Take care of your body. What physical activities did you do this week?

Week 27

"Finally, brothers, whatever is true, whatever is honorable, whatever is just, whatever is pure, whatever is lovely, whatever is gracious, if there is any excellence and if there is anything worthy of praise, think about these things."

Philippians 4:8

What is this passage saying to me today?

Other scripture that can help me think about this:

Think about this during your moment of silence:

What are the "irreducible minimums" or "non-negotiable items" in my life (for example, dinner with my family no fewer than four nights each week, no more than X hours on my computer after X:00 at night)?

If I don't have any, what should they be?

What I'm learning during my moments of silence this week:

Given what I've learned from scripture and during my moments of silence this week, what am I going to do about it and when am I going to get it done (put it on a calendar if you need to)?

Take care of your body. What physical activities did you do this week?

Week 28

Date:

___

"Proclaim the word; be persistent whether it is convenient
or inconvenient; convince, reprimand, encourage through
all patience and teaching."

2 Timothy 4:2

___

What is this passage saying to me today?

Other scripture that can help me think about this:

Think about this during your moment of silence:

How do I mentor or set a good example for others?

Who could benefit the most from the knowledge I have?

How should I be sharing that with him or her?

When will I do it?

What I'm learning during my moments of silence this week:

Given what I've learned from scripture and during my moments of silence this week, what am I going to do about it and when am I going to get it done (put it on a calendar if you need to)?

Take care of your body. What physical activities did you do this week?

Week 29

Date:

"Watch carefully then how you live, not as foolish persons
but as wise, making the most of the opportunity, because
the days are evil. Therefore, do not continue in ignorance,
but try to understand what is the will of the Lord."

Ephesians 5:15-17

What is this passage saying to me today?

Other scripture that can help me think about this:

Think about this during your moment of silence:

A lot of people have "to do" lists. What are the time-wasting
things I do every day that should be on my "not to do" list?

What I'm learning during my moments of silence this week:

Given what I've learned from scripture and during my moments of silence this week, what am I going to do about it and when am I going to get it done (put it on a calendar if you need to)?

Take care of your body. What physical activities did you do this week?

Week 30

Date:
_____

"Blessed are you when they insult you and persecute you and
utter every kind of evil against you (falsely) because of me."

Matthew 5:11

_____

What is this passage saying to me today?

Other scripture that can help me think about this:

Think about this during your moment of silence:

What values do I have that I cannot compromise?

What do I do when I'm asked to do so?

What I'm learning during my moments of silence this week:

Given what I've learned from scripture and during my moments of silence this week, what am I going to do about it and when am I going to get it done (put it on a calendar if you need to)?

Take care of your body. What physical activities did you do this week?

Week 31

Date:
_____

"And whoever does not provide for relatives and especially family members has denied the faith and is worse than an unbeliever."

1 Timothy 5:8

_____

What is this passage saying to me today?

Other scripture that can help me think about this:

Think about this during your moment of silence:

What member of my family really needs more from me?

How and when will I help him or her?

What I'm learning during my moments of silence this week:

Given what I've learned from scripture and during my moments of silence this week, what am I going to do about it and when am I going to get it done (put it on a calendar if you need to)?

Take care of your body. What physical activities did you do this week?

Week 32

Date:

_____

"And the king will say to them in reply,
'Amen I say to you, whatever you did for one
of these least brothers of mine, you did for me.'"

Matthew 25:40

_____

What is this passage saying to me today?

Other scripture that can help me think about this:

Think about this during your moment of silence:

How can I better serve my community?

When will I start?

What I'm learning during my moments of silence this week:

Given what I've learned from scripture and during my moments of silence this week, what am I going to do about it and when am I going to get it done (put it on a calendar if you need to)?

Take care of your body. What physical activities did you do this week?

Week 33

Date:

_____

"As each one has received a gift, use it to serve
one another as good stewards of God's varied grace."

1 Peter 4:10

_____

What is this passage saying to me today?

Other scripture that can help me think about this:

Think about this during your moment of silence:

What talents do I have that not many people in my world know about?

How can I use these talents to better serve others?

What I'm learning during my moments of silence this week:

Given what I've learned from scripture and during my moments of silence this week, what am I going to do about it and when am I going to get it done (put it on a calendar if you need to)?

Take care of your body. What physical activities did you do this week?

Week 34

Date:
_____

"Call to me, and I will answer you; I will tell you great
things beyond the reach of your knowledge."

Jeremiah 33:3

_____

What is this passage saying to me today?

Other scripture that can help me think about this:

Think about this during your moment of silence:

What is the toughest choice I'm facing right now?

Am I getting input from all the right people before
having to make this choice?

What I'm learning during my moments of silence this week:

Given what I've learned from scripture and during my moments of silence this week, what am I going to do about it and when am I going to get it done (put it on a calendar if you need to)?

Take care of your body. What physical activities did you do this week?

Week 35

Date:

_____

"The heart of the intelligent acquires knowledge,
and the ear of the wise seeks knowledge."

Proverbs 18:15

_____

What is this passage saying to me today?

Other scripture that can help me think about this:

Think about this during your moment of silence:

What is the one thing I really want to learn?

How will I seek that out?

What I'm learning during my moments of silence this week:

Given what I've learned from scripture and during my moments of silence this week, what am I going to do about it and when am I going to get it done (put it on a calendar if you need to)?

Take care of your body. What physical activities did you do this week?

Week 36

Date:

_____

"Then he took the bread, said the blessing, broke it, and gave it to
them, saying, 'This is my body, which will be given for you; do this
in memory of me.' And likewise the cup after they had eaten, saying,
'This cup is the new covenant in my blood, which will be shed for you.'"

Luke 22:19-20

_____

What is this passage saying to me today?

Other scripture that can help me think about this:

Think about this during your moment of silence:

What would I like someone to say about me at my funeral?

Is what I want said about me a reality already?

If not, what do I need to do in order to make it so?

What I'm learning during my moments of silence this week:

Given what I've learned from scripture and during my moments of silence this week, what am I going to do about it and when am I going to get it done (put it on a calendar if you need to)?

Take care of your body. What physical activities did you do this week?

Week 37

Date:

"Whatever you do, do from the heart, as for the Lord and not for others, knowing that you will receive from the Lord the due payment of the inheritance; be slaves of the Lord Christ."

Colossians 3:23-24

What is this passage saying to me today?

Other scripture that can help me think about this:

Think about this during your moment of silence:

On what should I be working harder?

What do I feel is blocking me from working harder in this area?

What I'm learning during my moments of silence this week:

Given what I've learned from scripture and during my moments of silence this week, what am I going to do about it and when am I going to get it done (put it on a calendar if you need to)?

Take care of your body. What physical activities did you do this week?

Week 38

Date:
_____

> "Therefore, confess your sins to one another and pray
> for one another, that you may be healed. The fervent prayer
> of a righteous person is very powerful."
>
> *James 5:16*

_____

What is this passage saying to me today?

Other scripture that can help me think about this:

Think about this during your moment of silence:

To whom do I need to apologize?

For what?

How and when will I deliver my apology?

What I'm learning during my moments of silence this week:

Given what I've learned from scripture and during my moments of silence this week, what am I going to do about it and when am I going to get it done (put it on a calendar if you need to)?

Take care of your body. What physical activities did you do this week?

Week 39

Date: _____

"Then Peter approaching asked him, 'Lord, if my brother sins against me, how often must I forgive him? As many as seven times?' Jesus answered, 'I say to you, not seven times but seventy-seven times.'"

Matthew 18:21-22

What is this passage saying to me today?

Other scripture that can help me think about this:

Think about this during your moment of silence:

Who needs my forgiveness?

How and when will I tell them that I've forgiven them?

What do I hope to accomplish by doing this?

What I'm learning during my moments of silence this week:

Given what I've learned from scripture and during my moments of silence this week, what am I going to do about it and when am I going to get it done (put it on a calendar if you need to)?

Take care of your body. What physical activities did you do this week?

Week 40

Date:

_____

"Find your delight in the LORD who will
give you your heart's desire."

Psalms 37:4

_____

What is this passage saying to me today?

Other scripture that can help me think about this:

Think about this during your moment of silence:

How do I define success?

Am I achieving that success now?

If not, how will I get there?

What I'm learning during my moments of silence this week:

Given what I've learned from scripture and during my moments of silence this week, what am I going to do about it and when am I going to get it done (put it on a calendar if you need to)?

Take care of your body. What physical activities did you do this week?

Week 41

Date:

_____

"Do not fear: I am with you; do not be anxious:
I am your God. I will strengthen you, I will help you,
I will uphold you with my victorious right hand."

Isaiah 41:10

_____

What is this passage saying to me today?

Other scripture that can help me think about this:

Think about this during your moment of silence:

What scares me more than anything else?

What can I do to overcome this fear?

What I'm learning during my moments of silence this week:

Given what I've learned from scripture and during my moments of silence this week, what am I going to do about it and when am I going to get it done (put it on a calendar if you need to)?

Take care of your body. What physical activities did you do this week?

Week 42

Date:
_____

"For by the grace given to me I tell everyone among you not to think
of himself more highly than one ought to think, but to think soberly,
each according to the measure of faith that God has apportioned."

Romans 12:3

_____

What is this passage saying to me today?

Other scripture that can help me think about this:

Think about this during your moment of silence:

In 50 words or less, how would I describe myself to a new neighbor
or co-worker?

Am I happy with that description?

If not, how can I change so that I can give a better description
in the future?

What I'm learning during my moments of silence this week:

Given what I've learned from scripture and during my moments of silence this week, what am I going to do about it and when am I going to get it done (put it on a calendar if you need to)?

Take care of your body. What physical activities did you do this week?

Week 43

Date:

"Brothers, I for my part do not consider myself to have taken possession. Just one thing: forgetting what lies behind but straining forward to what lies ahead, I continue my pursuit toward the goal, the prize of God's upward calling, in Christ Jesus."

Philippians 3:13-14

What is this passage saying to me today?

Other scripture that can help me think about this:

Think about this during your moment of silence:

When I think about my past, what do I need to let go?

What can I do to make that happen?

What I'm learning during my moments of silence this week:

Given what I've learned from scripture and during my moments of silence this week, what am I going to do about it and when am I going to get it done (put it on a calendar if you need to)?

Take care of your body. What physical activities did you do this week?

Week 44

Date: _____

"There is an appointed time for everything and a time
for every affair under the heavens."

Ecclesiastes 3:1

_____

What is this passage saying to me today?

Other scripture that can help me think about this:

Think about this during your moment of silence:

How do I feel about my work/life balance?

What can I do to make it better?

If I don't work, how do I feel about the balance of the things
that keep me occupied? What can I do to make it better?

Where should I be spending more or less of my time?

What I'm learning during my moments of silence this week:

Given what I've learned from scripture and during my moments of silence this week, what am I going to do about it and when am I going to get it done (put it on a calendar if you need to)?

Take care of your body. What physical activities did you do this week?

Week 45

Date:

"I recognized that there is nothing better than to rejoice and
do well during life. Moreover, that all can eat and drink and
enjoy the good of all their toil—this is a gift of God."

Ecclesiastes 3:12-13

What is this passage saying to me today?

Other scripture that can help me think about this:

Think about this during your moment of silence:

What is the current pace of my life? Am I okay with it?

If so, what do I need to do in order to maintain this pace?

If not, what do I need to add, change, or eliminate?

What I'm learning during my moments of silence this week:

Given what I've learned from scripture and during my moments of silence this week, what am I going to do about it and when am I going to get it done (put it on a calendar if you need to)?

Take care of your body. What physical activities did you do this week?

Week 46

Date: _____

"But when you pray, go to your inner room,
close the door, and pray to your Father in secret.
And your Father who sees in secret will repay you."

Matthew 6:6

What is this passage saying to me today?

Other scripture that can help me think about this:

Think about this during your moment of silence:

What am I doing to ensure that I am setting enough time
aside each day to be quiet and think?

What I'm learning during my moments of silence this week:

Given what I've learned from scripture and during my moments of silence this week, what am I going to do about it and when am I going to get it done (put it on a calendar if you need to)?

Take care of your body. What physical activities did you do this week?

Week 47

Date:

_____

"Hear my son, your father's instruction,
and reject not your mother's teaching."

Proverbs 1:8

_____

What is this passage saying to me today?

Other scripture that can help me think about this:

Think about this during your moment of silence:

What lesson did I learn in my childhood that I still use today?

Have I shared this with others?

What I'm learning during my moments of silence this week:

Given what I've learned from scripture and during my moments of silence this week, what am I going to do about it and when am I going to get it done (put it on a calendar if you need to)?

Take care of your body. What physical activities did you do this week?

Week 48

Date:

_____

"Know this, my dear brothers: everyone should be
quick to hear, slow to speak, slow to wrath, for the wrath
of a man does not accomplish the righteousness of God."

James 1:19-20

_____

What is this passage saying to me today?

Other scripture that can help me think about this:

Think about this during your moment of silence:

Who in my life should I be "talking at" less and "listening to" more?

How can I improve my ability to listen?

What I'm learning during my moments of silence this week:

Given what I've learned from scripture and during my moments of silence this week, what am I going to do about it and when am I going to get it done (put it on a calendar if you need to)?

Take care of your body. What physical activities did you do this week?

Week 49

Date:

"There is nothing concealed that will not be revealed, nor secret that will not be known. Therefore, whatever you have said in the darkness will be heard in the light, and what you have whispered behind closed doors will be proclaimed on the housetops."

Luke 12:2-3

What is this passage saying to me today?

Other scripture that can help me think about this:

Think about this during your moment of silence:

What is a secret that I have? Is there someone I should tell?

Would this do good or harm?

What I'm learning during my moments of silence this week:

Given what I've learned from scripture and during my moments of silence this week, what am I going to do about it and when am I going to get it done (put it on a calendar if you need to)?

Take care of your body. What physical activities did you do this week?

Week 50

"Do nothing out of selfishness or out of vainglory; rather, humbly regard others as more important than yourselves, each looking out not for his own interests, but [also] everyone for those of others."

Philippians 2:3-4

What is this passage saying to me today?

Other scripture that can help me think about this:

Think about this during your moment of silence:

It is said that life is 10% what happens to me and 90% how I react to it. In what areas of my life might I be reacting to something in a way that adversely affects myself or others?

What impact is my reaction having? What's stopping me from reacting differently and what can I do about that?

What I'm learning during my moments of silence this week:

Given what I've learned from scripture and during my moments of silence this week, what am I going to do about it and when am I going to get it done (put it on a calendar if you need to)?

Take care of your body. What physical activities did you do this week?

Week 51

Date:

_____

"I tell you, everyone who acknowledges me before
others the Son of Man will acknowledge before the angels
of God. But whoever denies me before others will be
denied before the angels of God."

Luke 12:8-9

_____

What is this passage saying to me today?

Other scripture that can help me think about this:

Think about this during your moment of silence:

Am I open with others about my faith?

If so, how am I sharing it with others?

If not, what should I be doing about it?

What I'm learning during my moments of silence this week:

Given what I've learned from scripture and during my moments of silence this week, what am I going to do about it and when am I going to get it done (put it on a calendar if you need to)?

Take care of your body. What physical activities did you do this week?

Week 52

Date:

_____

"Jesus looked at them and said, 'For human beings this
is impossible, but for God all things are possible.'"

Matthew 19:26

_____

What is this passage saying to me today?

Other scripture that can help me think about this:

Think about this during your moment of silence:

What is a risk that I've been unwilling to take?

What's stopping me from taking it?

What would be the benefit to me and those I love if I take it?

How will I feel if I never take this risk?

What I'm learning during my moments of silence this week:

Given what I've learned from scripture and during my moments
of silence this week, what am I going to do about it and when am
I going to get it done (put it on a calendar if you need to)?

Take care of your body. What physical activities did you do
this week?

Journal

Works Consulted

It is my intent to give credit for use of copyrighted material contained in this book. If such credit has inadvertently been omitted, please contact me at kevin@oi-solutions.com so subsequent printings will contain the appropriate acknowledgment.

Made in the USA
Lexington, KY
21 December 2018